The Blind Beggar

Outside the city of Jericho sat a poor man. His name was Bartimaeus. He was a beggar. He could not work. He was blind. How sad not to be able to see at all!

Day by day he begged for money from anyone who passed by. But this day was different. A procession was going along the road near to where Bartimaeus was sitting. It was Jesus, followed by a large number of people.

Poor Bartimaeus could not see anything that was happening, but he could hear men talking. They were saying that it was Jesus who was passing by.

Soon Jesus and His friends were passing the very spot where Bartimaeus sat.

"Jesus, Thou Son of David, have mercy on me."

Who was this that was crying out so loudly? It was the poor, blind beggar, Bartimaeus.

Poor Bartimaeus knew that this wonderful Saviour, Jesus, could help him. He knew too

that no one else could. So he called loudly to Jesus for help.

"Hold your peace! Be quiet!" cried the people round about. They thought that Jesus would not want to be bothered with a beggar.

But do you know what the blind man did? He called for help to Jesus all the more! The others were not blind as he was. They did not feel their great need as he did.

And then a wonderful thing happened. Jesus, the Son of God, stood still. The beggar's cry made Him stop. He told the people to call Bartimaeus to Him. And Bartimaeus was so glad to come.

Then Jesus spoke most kindly to the blind man. He asked him what he would really like Him to do for him.

There could be only one answer for there was one thing that Bartimaeus wanted more than anything else. He wanted to be able to see.

So Bartimaeus humbly asked the Lord Jesus. He said, "Lord, that I might receive my sight." And Jesus in His great kindness and mercy did for him just what he wanted.

He made him see. What a wonderful thing took place that day!

So now the procession moved on—with an extra person joining in. Perhaps you can guess who it was? Yes, it was Bartimaeus. And, do you know, I think he would try to keep as close as possible to Jesus, who had done so much for him. Don't you? One thing we do know. As he went, he praised and blessed God. He was so thankful.

I wonder what you and I would answer should Jesus ask us what we would like Him to do for us more than anything else? Would it be to give us some wonderful present we have been longing for? Or would it be what we ask for in the little children's hymn?

"Let my sins be all forgiven,
  Bless the friends I love so well;
Take me when I die to heaven,
  Happy there with Thee to dwell."

You can read this story in the Bible in Mark, chapter 10, verses 46 to 52.

The Stilling of the Storm

It was evening by the Sea of Galilee. The sea was calm. Jesus told His disciples to get into a little ship and sail across to the other side. I am sure they felt very pleased when they knew that Jesus was coming with them. As they set sail, other little ships were sailing by their side.

Many of you girls and boys will know the verse:

"A little ship was on the sea,
    It was a pretty sight;
  It sailed along so pleasantly,
    And all was calm and bright."

But now see what a change was taking place. The sky grew dark. A storm was coming. The wind began to blow. Soon it was so strong that the sea was blown into the ship. The poor disciples were terrified— though really they should not have been as Jesus was with them in the ship.

Now the ship was full of water. It seemed that it must surely sink.

And what was Jesus doing? He was at the back of the ship—asleep! He was not afraid of the wind and the waves.

The frightened disciples woke Him up. "Master," they cried, "carest Thou not that we perish?"

Jesus stood up. Calmly He spoke to the wind and the sea. He said, "Peace, be still." He told the storm to be quiet. And the wind and waves and storm did just what they were told to do. They obeyed. Everything obeys the Lord—wind, sea, fire, rain, snow— everything! "There was a great calm."

The disciples were amazed. They knew Jesus was a real man, their Master and Friend. But they could see that He was more than just a man. He was also God.

"What kind of man is this?" they said to each other. "Even the wind and the sea obey His voice."

Now the sea was calm again, the disciples soon arrived safely at the other side of the lake. How glad they must have been to reach the shore without harm!

I wonder if you ever have to pray to this

wonderful Person? He is now in heaven, but still hears the cries of His people to help them and to save them.

You can read this story in Mark, chapter 4, verses 35 to 41.

The Money in the Fish's Mouth

One day a few men came up to Simon Peter. They were collecting money for God's house, the temple. They asked Peter if his Master, Jesus, would pay.

"Yes," said Peter. "He will."

Now Peter really should not have said this for Jesus is God's Son, and God's Son does not have to pay for His Father's house.

Soon afterwards Peter came into the house where Jesus was. Now Jesus knows everything, and He knew all that Peter had been doing and saying; and He knows all we say or do.

This time it was Jesus who asked a question. "What do you think, Simon? Do kings collect money from their own children, or from the people in their country?"

Simon Peter knew the answer to this. It was easy. He answered straight away. It was from the people. Kings would never collect from their own children.

"Then," answered Jesus, "the children are

free."

So Peter learned what he should have known before. He should have been more careful. Jesus was no ordinary person. He was the Son of God. God's Son did not need to pay the money for His Father's house.

But then Jesus spoke very gently and kindly. He said that they must not offend those men who were asking for the money. Then He told Peter to do a strange thing. He told him to go fishing and when he caught the first fish, to look in its mouth.

So Simon Peter went. He was used to fishing. Soon a fish was caught, and what do you think was in its mouth? A piece of money exactly enough to pay the temple money for both the Lord Jesus and Peter.

How did the fish come to have the money in its mouth? Did it swallow it? We do not know. But we do know that all creatures obey the Lord. The ravens took meat for Elijah. The lions did not bite Daniel. The snake did not hurt Paul. It was the Lord who saw that the money was there in the fish's mouth.

So Peter caught the fish, and the fish contained the money, and in this wonderful way the need was supplied and the temple money paid. Whatever the Lord's people need, for body or soul, He will supply. There is a beautiful verse:

"My God shall supply all your need according to His riches in glory by Christ Jesus."

You can read this story in Matthew, chapter 17, verses 24 to 27.

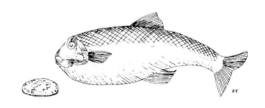

The Feeding of the Five Thousand

All day long Jesus had been teaching the people by the lake. It was now late. Evening was drawing near. The disciples thought it was time everyone went home.

"Master, send them away," said the disciples.

But how different were the thoughts of Jesus! His heart was full of kindness to the large crowd of people—five thousand men, as well as women and children.

"Give them all something to eat," said the Lord Jesus.

The disciples were just puzzled. Whatever could their Master mean? They had nothing to give to all those people to eat. Philip tried to reckon up how much it would cost to buy enough food. It just could not be done.

Then someone pointed out a little boy. Who he was we do not know, nor how old he was, nor why he had come. But this little boy was carrying five loaves of bread and two little fishes—something like our sardines.

Andrew told Jesus about him, but it seemed silly to think of beginning to feed the people with this little bit of food.

Then Jesus spoke. He told all the people to sit down on the thick, green grass. And they did just what they were told. It must have been a marvellous sight to see this great multitude all sitting down together when commanded by the Lord Jesus.

Jesus took the loaves and the fishes, but first He gave thanks to His Father in heaven. Just in the same way, we give thanks to God before we eat.

Then Jesus began to break the bread and fish into pieces. The disciples handed it round, and there was enough for every person there. They could each have as much as they wanted.

We wonder what the little boy thought, but we are not told. How amazing that Jesus should use a little child!

You would have thought that this was the end. But no! All the crumbs had to be gathered up. Jesus could so easily work a miracle, but we must not be careless or wasteful. The crumbs and pieces of fish left over filled twelve baskets—the large fishermen's baskets. We wonder if there was one basket full for each of the disciples?

Yes, Jesus can perform any miracle. He is Lord of all. He can forgive any sin, save any soul, answer any prayer.

Listen to Him speaking:

"Behold, I am the Lord, the God of all flesh. Is there anything too hard for Me?"

You can read about this miracle in each of the gospels—Matthew, chapter 14, verses 15 to 21; Mark 6, 35 to 44; Luke 9, 12 to 17; John 6, 5 to 14.

Here is a little prayer for before meals:

Lord, bless this food, and grant that we
May thankful for Thy mercies be;
Teach us to know by whom we're fed:
Bless us with Christ, the living Bread.

Jairus' Daughter

There was once a man named Jairus. He was not poor and blind like Bartimaeus. He was well-known. Probably he was rich. But he was very sad.

He had a little girl who was very ill. Jairus was sure she was going to die. We are not told her name—only that she was twelve years old.

Was there nothing that could be done?

People were saying that Jesus had arrived in the town. Jairus had heard that Jesus could do wonderful things. He knew He could make sick people better. So he ran and fell down at Jesus' feet, begging Him to help.

"My little daughter lies at the point of death," he said. "I pray Thee come."

And Jesus did not refuse him. He listened so kindly to him. Then immediately He started to go with him to the house where the poor little girl lay ill.

But what a disappointment! Someone else came for Jesus to help—a poor woman. And Jesus stopped, and talked with her, and helped her. But how anxious poor Jairus felt! Would Jesus get to his house in time? Or would it be too late?

Then he heard some sad news. What he feared had now happened. A message came saying, "Your little girl is dead." The messenger added what Jairus must have been feeling, "Why trouble the Master any further?" All poor Jairus' hopes were dashed.

But it was not too late! Listen to Jesus speaking. What wonderful words! "Be not afraid. Only believe." O, can the little girl be saved after all?

As Jesus and His disciples came near the house, they heard sounds of sadness. People were crying and weeping.

But Jesus knew what He was going to do. "She is not dead, but sleepeth," He said. How the people laughed at Him!

Then the Lord Jesus took the little girl's father and mother with Him. Together they entered the room where she lay. Now watch a miracle taking place. Jesus took her by the hand, and said, "Little girl, I say to you, arise." Yes, Jesus can even raise the dead.

To everyone's amazement, she got up and walked about the room. Jesus said, "Give her something to eat." She was not only alive, but hungry. All the people were astonished.

Nothing is too hard for the Lord Jesus. The most impossible things with Him are easy. He is now in heaven. He listens to our prayers. He still answers the prayers of His people as He answered the prayer of Jairus.

You can read this story in Mark, chapter 5, verses 21 to 43.

Healing the Leper

One day Jesus came down from a mountain where He had been teaching the people. Crowds of people followed Him.

Suddenly a strange thing happened. Who is this poor man coming up to Jesus? He is very ill. His hands and legs and body look very sore. Some of his fingers seem to be no longer there. He must have a dreadful illness. Yes, he is a leper.

How sad it must have been to be a leper! No one was allowed near him. He must leave his friends and family. If he wants something to eat, it must be left for him. People do not want to come anywhere near him in case they should become lepers as well.

Now look! What is this leper doing? Why, he is falling down at Jesus' feet. He is worshipping Him. Now he is talking to Jesus. Listen to what he is saying. He is telling Jesus that he knows He can make him better—if only He will!

And Jesus did not run away from him, or

speak unkindly to him, or send him away. Have you noticed that Jesus never refused help to those who asked Him? But this was very, very hard. No one could make a leper better. The doctors could not cure lepers.

"And Jesus put forth His hand and touched him." Then He spoke, so simply and yet so kindly. He said, "I will. Be thou clean."

What power there is in Jesus' word! What love! What kindness! Jesus had done what no one else could do. The poor leper was completely better, and made better straight away. How many wonderful things Jesus did by just touching! You and I have to try so hard to do many little things, but these hard things were easy to Jesus. It was so easy for Jesus to make the leper's skin clean and better by just touching it. And Jesus was pleased to do it.

Perhaps you have heard people pray to God to make them clean. Whatever do they mean? Are they lepers? They mean that just as the leper was ugly and his skin rough and dreadful, so because of our sin we need Jesus to heal us and make us clean from our sins.

There is a very beautiful verse. Try to remember it, and may God teach you what it means:

"The blood of Jesus Christ His Son cleanseth us from all sin."

You can read this story in Mark, chapter 1, verses 40 to 45.

The Man Let Down Through the Roof

There was once a poor, sick man. He was very weak. He could not move his arms or his legs. He had to lie helpless all day on his little bed.

But you will be glad to know that this poor man had four good friends. One day his four friends heard that Jesus was preaching in a house in the town. They knew that Jesus could make him better. So they picked up the poor man's bed—it would be very light—and carried him through the streets to bring him to Jesus. What a blessing to have friends like this!

But when they got there, they were disappointed. The house was crowded with people, even outside the doors. They could not get anywhere near Jesus. Crowds had come from far and near to listen to the blessed words the Lord Jesus spoke.

What could the four men do now? Should they give up and go back home? No, they were real friends and would not give up easily. They hoped that this was the day when their sick friend would be made better. Was there anything they could do?

So they thought out a plan. They carried their friend on his bed up the steps that led onto the flat roof of the house. It must have been hard work but they did not mind. Then they made a hole in the tiles on the roof. Through the hole they let the poor man down just where Jesus was.

What a surprise to the crowd down below in the house! What was that noise in the ceiling? And why was this hole appearing? And now whatever was coming down from above? How strange to see the little bed let down just where Jesus was speaking!

Jesus was not angry. He was very pleased. He looked kindly at the poor man and said to him, "Son, thy sins be forgiven thee." What a joyful sound! All his sins forgiven! But what about his illness?

Now there were some enemies of Jesus in the crowd. They were angry. They began to grumble. They thought, "No one can forgive sins but God." And Jesus knew all the unkind things they were thinking. Then Jesus spoke. "Which is easier," He said, "to say, Your sins are forgiven, or to say, Rise, take up your bed, and walk?"

He then turned to the poor man and said to him, "Rise, take up your bed, and go to your house." And to everyone's amazement the man got up, picked up his little bed, and walked away. You can guess what he did as he went. Yes, he praised God with all his heart. He was cured. But even more wonderful, the Son of God had forgiven him and blessed him.

Jesus still has power to forgive sin. He is still able to save. May the Holy Spirit teach us our need to be forgiven.

"If we say that we have no sin, we deceive ourselves, and the truth is not in us. If we confess our sins, He is faithful and just to forgive us our sins, and to cleanse us from all unrighteousness."

You can read this story in Mark, chapter 2, verses 1 to 12.

The Wonderful Catch of Fish

A few of Jesus' disciples were wondering what to do. Strange things had been happening to them. Their Lord and Master, Jesus, had been taken from them and put to death on the cross. This had made them very, very sad. Then He had risen from the dead. He had come back to life. They had talked with Him. They knew He was alive.

But now things were different. He was not with them all the time as before. What should they do?

"I'm going fishing," said Peter.

"We will come with you," answered the others.

So they got into a boat and sailed out onto the sea. They threw their fishing net down into the water. Soon it was night. They waited for the fishes to come all night long. But when morning came they had caught no fish at all. Not a single one.

Day dawned over the Sea of Galilee. And the disciples sailed back to the shore with their empty net.

As they neared the land, they could see a man standing on the shore. They did not know who he was. He was a stranger.

Suddenly the stranger called to them. He asked them if they had any fish.

"No," they said. And we wonder if they said it crossly after their disappointment.

"Then," said the stranger, "throw your net on the other side of the boat."

Who was this stranger? Why was he telling them what to do? Anyway, they did as they were told. Immediately their net was full of fishes. Do you know how many they caught? A hundred and fifty-three.

But now the disciples were beginning to think. Who *was* this stranger? Suddenly John whispered to Peter, "It is the Lord." How thrilled Peter was to hear this! Without more ado he jumped over the side of the ship into the water to swim to Jesus—while the other disciples followed, dragging the heavy net full of fishes.

As soon as they reached land, they found that the Lord Jesus had made something for them to eat. Jesus had bread waiting for them and fish He had cooked over a fire. How kind and thoughtful! And how welcome to the tired disciples!

Then Jesus dined with them, and afterwards talked with them. How pleased they were to have Him with them once more! They rejoiced that their Lord was alive. Yes, they knew that Jesus had performed His greatest miracle of all—dying and rising again.

Jesus is now in heaven. He says, "I am He that liveth, and was dead; and behold, I am alive for evermore. Amen."

You can read this story in John, chapter 21, verses 1 to 14.